The Shirley Booth & Bill Baker Story

By Jim Manago

"For Bill, His Pinup Girl:
The Shirley Booth & Bill Baker Story"

Copyright @2010 Jim Manago

All Rights Reserved.

No part of this book may be reproduced in any form or by any means, electronic, mechanical, digital, photocopying or recording, except for the inclusion in a review, without permission in writing from the publisher.

The photographs and paintings in this book, including the cover photos, are not to be reproduced in any fashion without written permission.
Any unauthorized reproduction is a violation of copyright law.

Published in the USA by:
Jim & Donna Manago Books
http://shirleybooth.info

ISBN 978-0-615-42181-0

First edition

Book and cover design by D. Scott Lyttle

This Book is Dedicated to
Shirley Booth's sister, Jean Ford Coe
February 14, 1914 – January 23, 2010

In Loving Memory

Contents

Foreword: My Aunt Shirley 5

Preface 8

Acknowledgements 10

List of Illustrations 12

A Story of Love… 13

Postscript 27

The Photographs and Paintings 29

Credits 68

Appendix

The Farmhouse Today 71

By the Beautiful Sea 73

The Merv Griffin Interview 77

Foreword: My Aunt Shirley

by Leslie Sodaro

For as long as I can remember, my mother Jean said that her sister Shirley Booth (Aunt Shirley) had looked out for her. Aunt Shirley was 16 years older than my mother. Aunt Shirley (then Thelma) was the apple of her mother Virginia's eye; all of Aunt Shirley's teachers in school adored her, it was a tough road for my mother to travel. When my mother was 15, her mother Virginia died. Aunt Shirley stepped up for my mother. Aunt Shirley already had done this for my mother when she was a child as she did for her own mother when Virginia got divorced years earlier.

In 1949 to 1950, we were living in the Florida Keys in Marathon when my parents' marriage ended. Aunt Shirley told my mother to pack up my brother Jon and me, so that we can come back to New York. So, thanks to Aunt Shirley, we three settled into the house on McCoun's Lane in Glen Head, Long Island. The house still stands, but the area is so expensive that neither my mother nor I could afford it. We had lived near that town before we went to Florida.

Aunt Shirley engaged my mother as her secretary, and my mother would make the trip in to 'the city' (New York) from Glen Head three times a week until Aunt Shirley left to go to California to film *Hazel*. Aunt Shirley was kind enough to allow my mother and me to stay in Glen Head until I finished high school. My brother Jon had graduated five years earlier, and he entered the Air Force.

Then we moved to California when Jon returned from the Air Force. Aunt Shirley was on hiatus from *Hazel*, and she stayed in her Cape Cod house. She allowed us to stay in her Beverly Hills house on Beaumont Drive. We stayed there for a few months until our house in West Los Angeles was ready for us to move into. Our house happened to be across from the one owned by Edie Adams and her late husband, Ernie Kovacs. Sylvester Stallone subsequently purchased the Kovacs' house.

Although my mother worked for her until Aunt Shirley retired, Jon and I did not see that much of Aunt Shirley.

One year Aunt Shirley spent a Christmas Day dinner with us: my mother, Jon, his wife Maureen, my first husband Steve, his parents, Lorraine and Joe, Steve's sister Gina and her husband Gary. The dinner was wonderful. Aunt Shirley kept the entire table entertained with stories complete with accents. At some point during the meal, Aunt Shirley noticed that Gary had not eaten his sweet potato skins...at which point she asked, "Are you going to eat those?" He responded, "No." Aunt Shirley swept them off his plate and ate them to everyone's surprise, except to my mother and me.

I remember one trip up to Chatham, Massachusetts with my mother when my Aunt Shirley drove us to her first house on Chatham Bars Avenue. Later my Aunt sold that house because it was too large. She then bought a smaller house that she lived in until she died.

Never the greatest driver, Aunt Shirley tended to drive fast. I was sitting in the back seat. At some point, Aunt Shirley motioned to me to look at the cranberry bogs. I noticed that my mother, who was sitting in the passenger seat stiffen and continue to look straight forward...not at the cranberry bogs...because Aunt Shirley WAS looking at the bogs...and not the road. Obviously we all survived, but my mother would every so often say to me "remember those cranberry bogs?" and we would both laugh.

On the few occasions when my mother and I visited Shirley at the Chatham Bars house, we always had a good time. As a great hostess, Aunt Shirley had wonderfully interesting friends who would visit her.

My Aunt Shirley was a delight and loved dearly by the

whole family. As a truly kind human being, she watched over my mother Jean, my brother Jon and me making sure that we were taken care of and alright. Her generosity has enabled my mother to enjoy her later years without stress and worry. To Aunt Shirley's wonderful energy out there in the universe, I say THANK YOU!"

Preface

I told actress Shirley Booth's amazing story in *Love is the Reason for it All: The Shirley Booth Story*, published in 2008 by BearManor Media.

My biography explained that in the Broadway musical *A Tree Grows in Brooklyn*, Shirley exuberantly sang a song called "Love is the Reason for it All," by Arthur Schwartz and Dorothy Fields. That song humorously recognizes the reality of love: if it says anything, it tells of the trouble love causes. If something could explain why Shirley went through all the troubles of her life, and why she gave so much of herself as a performer, then this might be it. Audiences loved her, and this resulted from her intense love for audiences. Her need for love and her wish to give love is truly the reason for her whole career.

Over a year after my biography's release, I received a comment from Shirley's niece Leslie Sodaro after she discovered my blog (http://shirleybooth.info). Until this time, no one seemed to know the whereabouts of Shirley's closest relatives.

I learned that Shirley's only sibling, a younger sister, Jean Ford Coe, was still alive and living in a retirement home in Forest Grove, Oregon. Jean's daughter Leslie explained that her mother's aging had taken some toll. Although Jean's memories of some things were lost due to several strokes, she was still quite functional despite her 95-plus years.

I am glad that Jean had the opportunity to hear my biography of her famous sister read to her by staff members. Interestingly, Jean never knew that Shirley's birth certificate, which appeared in my book, revealed her birth name as 'Marjory.' She knew Shirley as simply 'Thelma.'

Soon after that initial contact, I had asked Leslie if she had any family photographs of her mom Jean and her Aunt Shirley. Unfortunately, there are no pictures of them together. This is because Jean was "unlike her photogenic sister, [so] she hated to have her picture taken." In addition, Shirley's parents (A.J. and Virginia) were not much into photography – so no photos of them exist. Finally, there are no photos of Shirley together with niece Leslie or her late nephew Jon.

When her Aunt Shirley's second husband, Bill Baker Jr., tragically died in 1951 at the age of forty-three, Leslie was still a baby. Therefore, she has no recollection of meeting her Uncle Bill.

The best news came when Leslie located forty photographs in the family's collection. She also found three paintings, two by Bill and one by Shirley. Most importantly, Leslie was kind enough to share them, first with me, and now with the rest of the world. When I saw these pictures of Shirley, in particular the pin-up shot given to her husband serving in World War II, I knew it would surprise her fans the most. I wanted everyone to see these never-before-seen photos. That was one of two reasons for the genesis of this small book of love...

The other reason for writing this book is the fact that I knew my first biography said little about the brief marriage of Shirley Booth to her second husband. The uncertainty brought on by his service in the war stifled their blossoming love during the darkness of World War II. Although the couple would be joyfully reunited after the war ended, within a short time, Shirley and Bill's life on their farm would take its toll.

Love is not always so easy, as indicated by that excellent Schwartz & Fields' song. This is the story of that bittersweet time in Shirley's life when she found and loved a compatible mate - her 'Bill,' only to tragically lose him.

My hope is that my book will provide a better understanding of this first happy and then sad period in the astounding career and personal life of Shirley Booth.

Jim Manago
September 2010

Acknowledgements

This book would not be possible without the photographs and paintings provided by Shirley Booth's niece and surviving next of kin, Leslie Sodaro. I offer my heartfelt thanks to her for making this book possible.

To supplement this follow-up book to my first study of Shirley, I took the liberty of publishing for the first time ever the entire interview Shirley gave in 1963. Her storytelling ability is clearly evidenced in this rare though disappointingly short exchange on *The Merv Griffin Show*. A special thanks is due to Phil Gries, Archival Television Audio, Inc. for audio taping that priceless program, among so many others in his collection. Phil did this at a time when even television stations were not saving copies of their own programs. If they did keep copies, they now usually refuse to share them with researchers.

This project of publishing these unseen photographs and telling the story of Shirley and Bill entailed the assistance of many individuals. My appreciation goes to Dr. Bahij Madany, the current owner since 1967 of Shirley and Bill's Bucks County property. Although my diligent efforts proved fruitless to locate any photos of the property as it looked when Shirley & Bill lived there in the late 1940's, Dr. Madany took time from his very busy schedule to generously share everything he could about the property as it now exists.

Dick Drury, and others from the 100th Infantry Division Association, offered information about Bill's military service.

I owe a debt of gratitude to the German writer and Nazi camp and prison survivor Friedrich Schlotterbeck for his remarkable 1947 story, *The Darker the Night, The Brighter the Stars*. That translated book has offered me a priceless perspective to the World War II period. With the exception of his niece, Schlotterbeck's entire family – father, mother, sister, brother -

20 in all – "suffered indescribably" the brutalities inflicted, and then were killed in revenge by the Gestapo.

I offer thanks to the following people for their invaluable support for this project: Stephen White for copy editing; Jeff Marshall from the Heritage Conservancy for helping me locate the address and current owner of Shirley and Bill's property in Newtown, Pennsylvania; Beth Lander and Donna Humphrey from the Spruance Library in Doylestown, Pennsylvania for newspaper clippings; and Katie from AskArt for auction records to Shirley's paintings.

My utmost gratitude extends to Scott Lyttle for providing his exceptional skill as this book's designer.

Finally, for her valuable advice, as well as her assistance in researching and editing, I thank my partner Donna Manago.

List of Illustrations

- Front cover: Wallet-size hand-colored Pin-up glamour shot of Shirley Booth, given to her husband during World War II, 1944.
- 4X6 B/W – Shirley Booth lounging on ship's deck, circa 1930's.
- 8X10 B/W – Shirley Booth in dressing room for *My Sister Eileen*, circa 1940.
- 8X10 B/W – Portrait of Corp. William H. Baker Jr., 100th Army Division.
- Cover photo of Pinup reproduced in B/W, 1944.
- Backside of cover photo reproduced in B/W, 1944.
- 8X10 B/W – Shirley Booth with Bill, admiring his painting.
- Painting by Bill Baker, Still Life depicting View Outside of Window, oil, unsigned.
- Painting by Bill Baker, Still Life depicting Seascape, oil, signed "William, H. Baker."
- Painting by Shirley Booth, Still Life depicting Snow Scene, oil, signed "Shirley Booth, 1954."
- 2 photos, 3X5 B/W – Shirley Booth in dress from *A Tree Grows in Brooklyn*, location unknown, 1951.
- Fourteen photos, 3X5 B/W – Audience member's view showing stage with Shirley Booth and cast performing in Broadway production of *By the Beautiful Sea*, 1954.
- Telegram informing Shirley of her Golden Globe Award, February 20, 1953.
- Theatre ticket ORDERGRAM for *By the Beautiful Sea*.
- Donaldson Award for *By the Beautiful Sea*.
- Bill & Shirley's Property in Bucks County, Pennsylvania, as it appears today, 2010.
- 'Roadie' and Leslie Sodaro (Shirley Booth's niece).
- Back Cover: Color view of two paintings by Bill Baker. Color picture of Shirley Booth & Bill Baker's Bucks County property as it appears today.

A Story of Love...

That first night in [the] concentration camp I thought again and again of the inscription on the gravestone of one of the murdered comrades: "The Darker the Night, the Brighter the Stars." And I recovered the courage that had oozed out of me.

- Friedrich Schlotterbeck
The Darker the Night, The Brighter the Stars

Shirley Booth, the celebrated actress of stage, screen, radio and television, probably best remembered today as television's maid *Hazel*, had an unusual life from 1946 to early 1951. During this period, she enjoyed being a farmer's wife on a working dairy farm in Bucks County, Pennsylvania.

However, if one were to go back a few years earlier, you would find that the situation did not appear so stress-free...

The story in this book is just a glimpse into the little-known life of a quite successful actress during a precarious period in the history of the world. Her career had been flourishing by 1942, but her personal life had reached a crisis that might have shattered her totally. Suddenly her famed marriage to a creative and career-boosting husband Ed Gardner ended in a divorce, and her life edged closer to complete breakdown.

Besides that, the world around her seemed to be heading into near-total annihilation. Simultaneously with each passing day, the Allies were fighting an intensifying struggle to end a bloody and horrendous war. The free world needed saving from the domination by two countries, Germany and Japan. Everywhere, daily reports of death and destruction had to unnerve anyone.

However, through it all, the words that German resistance leader Friedrich Schlotterbeck spoke about in his story of his imprisonment in a Nazi camp for over ten years, provided a remarkable metaphor. "The Darker the Night, the Brighter the Stars," truly gives one a glimmer of hope. In the midst of this night world, a world at war, and within the dark world of the inner heartbreak of divorce, comes the unfathomable possibility and reality of a new and much better love.

The hope that grows from this blossoming love surely cannot mitigate the outer insanity that was omnipresent in the world then. Nevertheless, I am certain that many such glimmers of brightness sprang up throughout the world at that time. They gave countless people reason for a brighter and better tomorrow. Here is just one story of true love – that love shared between Shirley Booth and Bill Baker...

Shirley Booth, born as Marjory Ford, on August 30, 1898 in upper Manhattan to Albert Ford and Virginia Wright, had no real formal training in acting. She honed her craft by spending most of her career on the stage. Her relentless perseverance starting in stock and repertory theatre began at the age of twelve.

Not only is she credited with appearing in over thirty Broadway shows and hundreds of stock theatre shows all over the U.S.A. and Canada – most to great critical acclaim, Shirley received countless awards for her fine stage acting, including three Tony's.

She traveled extensively throughout the United States. Early on, she alternated her Broadway shows with supporting player parts in various theatre company productions. In 1925, her first Broadway show, *Hell's Bells*, co–starred the then unknown Humphrey Bogart.

Ten years later, she achieved her first notable Broadway role when she played a gun moll in the long-running comedy *Three Men on a Horse*. Shirley would go on to offer some of her best acting on the stage; including playing the reporter in *The Philadelphia Story*, Ruth in *My Sister Eileen*, and the teacher of a

Nazi-indoctrinated boy in *Tomorrow the World*.

In addition, she was a big hit with radio audiences for playing Miss Duffy, the daughter of the bar owner in *Duffy's Tavern*. These successes were shared and augmented by her husband Ed Gardner. This is especially true of *Duffy's Tavern* since Ed produced, directed, wrote and starred in the show.

Her efforts to make Ed happy in their marriage (1929 – 1943), included giving up her Broadway career for a year and moving to the West Coast so Ed could do his Hollywood radio productions. Nonetheless, Ed would finally ask Shirley for a divorce in 1942 because he fell in love with another woman. In shock, she entered the Broadway dressing room for her dramatic production, *Tomorrow the World* practically in a trance. Simply put, Shirley admitted that she was the closest to having a nervous breakdown at this time of her life.

Shirley explained to *The Herald Tribune*: "Suddenly I was afraid to face an audience. I can't describe how horrible it was to go out in front of a thousand people and I feel my insides jerking, sweat pouring out of my palms, completely unsure for the first and last time in my life. I fought it. I went to all kinds of doctors, but the only medicine that seemed to work was the hardest to take – just keep going out there."

However, within a month after her divorce to Ed was finalized in August of 1943, Shirley married again. Not being a love on the rebound, this time she had found her soul mate, and those years would be the happiest years of her life indeed.

Almost as if she learned something from being married to the coarser and abusive Ed Gardner, the man Shirley would marry this time around was the quieter and educated Corporal William Hogg Baker Jr., a noncommissioned army officer with the 100th Division. He would enter the service as a warrant officer - not entering officer status by a writ of being commissioned - but by a warrant. The rank of warrant officer is above enlistees, but it is below the commissioned officer.

Shirley simply referred to him as "Bill." He was born in 1907 in Hannibal, Missouri, and he achieved success as an investment banker before his service in the Army.

Bill Baker's family had attained social prominence in Montclair, New Jersey as indicated by plenty of press coverage over the years. Bill's father, William Hogg Baker, had been the president of the Merritt-Chapman & Scott Corporation, a salvage and marine construction company, responsible for the salvaging of the Normandie. He died in 1932 from a heart ailment at 52 years old.

Bill's mother, Catherine Elizabeth Baker, received her music training in Italy and performed in the U.S. and abroad as a piano and violin concert artist before she married in 1906. Catherine died in 1938, after being ill for six years, at the age of 56 years old.

Bill graduated Princeton University in 1929.

In 1930, the society page of *The New York Times*, announced that Bill, along with his father, mother, and sister Edith went to their summer home at Watch Hill, Rhode Island.

Much coverage to social events involved the William H. Baker's of Montclair. For instance, Bill's sister Sarah Jane Baker would marry David Lindsay 3d of Wilmington, Delaware in 1929. The papers announced that they had a son in 1932. Then Sarah would sue for a divorce in 1936. The following year Bill, listed as living then in Long Beach, California, would give Sarah into her second marriage – this time to William George Volkmann, Jr. of Piedmont, California.

By 1934, Bill was elected to be director at his late father's company (Merritt-Chapman & Scott Corporation), succeeding his uncle, Franklin Baker Jr. Bill also reportedly worked at some point with the New York Trust Company and for Loomis-Sayles, Inc.

The story goes that Bill first met Shirley while she vacationed in Nantucket with husband Ed. Later, when word circulated that Shirley was to be divorced, Bill contacted her. Soon their love flourished. Several months passed before the papers announced that Bill planned to marry Shirley on September 24, 1943.

Bill received a four-day furlough from the 100th Infantry Division located in Fort Jackson, South Carolina, which allowed him to marry Shirley. The Rev. Norris L. Tibbetts, from the Riverside Church, performed the ceremony at the home of Bill's aunt, Mrs. Franklin Baker Jr. Shirley had been appearing on Broadway in *Tomorrow the World*. When she left the show for those few days, Mildred Todd replaced her.

The enlistment records of December 14, 1942 indicate that Bill had signed up for service a full nine months before marrying Shirley. His unit of the 100th Division was the HQ Battery, 375th Field Artillery Battalion. The Army assigned him the serial number 3268328. He listed his occupation as "salesman, insurance."

The men in the 100th Division were trained from 1943 to early 1944 in the Tennessee mountains. They then finished training at Fort Bragg in North Carolina. Finally, they sailed to France in October 1944, where they would spend over five months in fierce combat to push the Germans out of Eastern France. Bill received the Bronze Star Medal for his service.

When Shirley finished her run in *Tomorrow the World* (the same show that Ed had announced his decision to seek a divorce), she is reported to have gone to the South to be close-by while Bill was training at various camp locations. Also, while Bill was in training and overseas, Shirley kept busy jitterbugging and entertaining the troops nightly at New York City's Stagedoor Canteen.

Just before *Tomorrow the World* closed on June 17, 1944, *The New York Times* published a classified ad that read as follows in the June 2, 1944 issue:

LOST: Engagement ring solitaire. 1 large stone, 6 small ones in cab vicinity Sardi's restaurant; reward. Shirley Booth, Ethel Barrymore Theatre.

Whether she recovered the ring or not is unknown.

Bill supported Shirley's next pursuit - an offer to star in her first musical on Broadway called *Hollywood Pinafore*. Unfortunately, the show did not last long; as it began on May 31, 1945, and it closed on July 14, 1945.

With the battalion officially inactivated on January 12, 1946 at Camp Patrick Henry in Newport News, Virginia, and the war now over, Bill would return home to become Shirley's manager. Now Shirley, for the second time in her life, retired to being a wife and homemaker. With their joint savings, they bought Wind Race Estate, a dairy farm in Buck's County, Pennsylvania, complete with cows, sheep and chickens.

As strange as it may seem, Bill the college graduate and successful broker wanted to be a farmer. That was one of his dreams. His return from the atrocities of World War II spurred him to find the solace that he envisioned in the dream of being a farmer.

Shirley had already achieved recognition and accolades for a number of successful Broadway shows in the late 1930's and early 1940's. Although she loved being a stage actress, she also seemed to be perfectly matched to Bill in his pursuit of country living since she loved animals and wanted the serenity that homemaking would provide her. Shirley shared Bill's shyness, and just like him seemed well-suited to the private world of being a homebody.

Shirley and Bill's new home, a remodeled stone farmhouse, was located at 72 Maple Lane in Newtown, Pennsylvania. According to deed records, the property was purchased on September 3, 1946, which indicates that Francis E. and Emma E. Snively sold a 62-acre farm to William and Shirley Baker of New York (deed book 793, page 52). Just two weeks after their purchase, Bill conveyed his interest to his wife on September 17, 1946 (deed book 795, page 218).

Years later, a newspaper noted incorrectly that the farm was in upstate New York. Shirley reportedly said: "I'm a farm girl to start with, you know. When my husband was alive, we used to have a farm of our own in upstate New York. We raised cows. We'd go to bed at nine in the evening and get up at dawn."

What were those years like down on the farm? Little is known about their country living. Although there are still farms in the area that date back to the 1940's, none of their neighbors, who knew the Bakers of Newtown, are still alive today. However, the couple apparently partook of the many responsibilities of the dairy farm. Bill did much of the heavy strenuous outdoor work, and Shirley kept very busy at interior decorating their farmhouse and caring for her farmer.

Besides the fact that Bill worked full-time as a farmer, he considered himself an artist. As can be expected from such a close-knit couple, Shirley took up painting as well. She later said that she learned to paint simply because Bill painted.

Shirley had settled down for the second time in her life to be a good wife. She had done this once before in 1938 when she gave up Broadway to please Ed Gardner. Then, however, Shirley soon missed Broadway too much to stay away more than a year.

In 1946, the situation was quite different. Shirley would not have to really give up Broadway. Now with her home in Bucks County, Shirley could still commute the 260 miles roundtrip to Broadway and the radio studios in New York City. Shirley's so-called 'sabbatical' from the Broadway stage and network radio studios was not so absolute because of Bucks County's proximity to New York.

Of the five Broadway shows she did from 1946 to 1951, the first three were embarrassing flops that closed quickly (*Land's End* in 1946, *The Men We Marry* in 1947, *Love Me Long* in 1949).

However, the shows that followed those flops were quite notable career high points; namely, *Goodbye, My Fancy* and *Come Back, Little Sheba.*

Goodbye, My Fancy ran from November 17, 1948 to December 24, 1949, which gave Shirley her first Tony for Best Supporting or Featured Actress.

The following year Shirley would appear in her most famous production of her entire stage career - the William Inge play *Come Back, Little Sheba.* At around the time she learned of the possibility of being in that production, Bill's health had already become a pressing concern. He had suffered a mild heart attack, and continued to have various setbacks thereafter.

Come Back, Little Sheba would make Shirley now famous throughout the world with numerous international awards, including a Cannes Award and her second Tony – finally for Best Actress. The play opened on February 15, 1950, running for 190 performances before closing on July 29, 1950.

Unfortunately, Bill's health troubles needed regular monitoring and follow-up. The farm proved too taxing on Bill's body. The only sensible thing for Shirley and Bill to do would be to sell the farm. Their move back to an apartment in New York City helped both of them. Shirley would not have to spend the four to five hours a day commuting, and Bill would be able to have better health care.

Shirley appeared in at least three early television shows while married to Bill, including the *March of Dimes Benefit Show* on January 22, 1949, and two episodes of the ABC's *Celebrity Time.* (August 28, 1949, and January 1, 1950).

In reviewing her radio broadcasting during the time when she lived down on the farm, it is apparent that Shirley proved herself a useful and productive voice talent.

Starting on September 29, 1946 and continuing until March 23, 1947, she was heard regularly on *The Eddie Bracken Show,* in a takeoff of her famous ditzy Miss Duffy character named

Betty Mahoney.

In addition, in 1946, she would be heard on a *Theater Guild on the Air* rendition of the production called "Broadway."

In 1947 and 1948, Shirley kept busy with a number of radio broadcasts, including a memorable telling of the story of famed lighthouse keeper Ida Lewis in *The Cavalcade of America* episode, "The Woman on Lime Rock." Her distinctive voice kept her returning to certain shows, such as Fred Allen's shows, *Here's to Veterans, Radio Reader's Digest*, and the *Theater Guild on the Air*. The latter series featured two reprised renditions of *Three Men on a Horse*, her big Broadway hit from 1935.

Unfortunately, all of the episodes featuring Shirley on Fred Allen's shows are supposedly "lost," or perhaps simply locked away in some collector's attic.

In what would quickly become Eve Arden's hit show, *Our Miss Brooks*, Shirley first tried out for the role of schoolteacher Connie Brooks. For some reason the entire cast, including Shirley, were not able to give a reading that was funny. It all sounded like a tragic drama – and this audition show never got broadcast.

Another episode of *The Cavalcade of America*, "The Man Who Took the Freedom Train," followed, and then Shirley would reprise her role from *My Sister Eileen* in radio's *The Ford Theatre*.

In 1949, Shirley reached a high point in her career with her Broadway hit show *Goodbye, My Fancy*. However, this did not stop her from being on various radio shows. She would be heard again on *Theater Guild on the Air* ("Street Scene"), and in a short-lived comedy called *Hogan's Daughter*. In the latter summer replacement show, Shirley would play Phyllis Hogan, a New York City working girl.

In 1950, she would be so absorbed by her tour de force *Come Back, Little Sheba*, from February to July, that she is credited with just one radio appearance in the *Theater Guild on the Air* production called 'The Milky Way," co-starring Danny Kaye.

Finally, between August of 1950 to February of 1951, Shirley did another episode of the *Theater Guild on the Air*. This time she reprised her big hit, *Come Back, Little Sheba*.

Shirley's next big success on Broadway after that latter watershed production would find her alone for the first time in over twenty years. Her tragic loss happened at the time when she began rehearsing for the second of her five Broadway musicals - her most memorable adaptation of Betty Smith's successful story, *A Tree Grows in Brooklyn*. It happened then, at the time she entered what would be a period of glowing success that her serenity with Bill would end.

From 1943 to 1945, the couple endured Bill's separation due to his involvement in serving our country. For several years from 1946 onward, they were reunited and lived happily together in Bucks County as soul mates. Their togetherness in the last year or so was spent back in a New York apartment as soon as Bill's health deteriorated significantly.

Inevitably, his family history had played an important part in predisposing Bill to heart problems. Bill's father had a fatal heart attack at an early age. At first, when they got married Shirley and Bill were unaware that he had heart problems too. Nevertheless, after the first mild heart attack, it became obvious that Bill could no longer do the strenuous work of a farmer as he had done, although Shirley had helped him recover.

Suddenly and sadly, Shirley's beloved husband Bill died of a heart attack in his sleep on March 4, 1951, at the age of 43. When Bill did not answer the telephone one morning in their New York City apartment at 25 West 54th Street– and Shirley went to check on him - she found him dead in bed.

Bill's surviving family was his brother Charles and his sister Edith Campaign.

Contrary to some reports later that the sale of their Bucks County property occurred after Bill's death, the effort to sell it had been underway the year before. The property was sold to

Robert and Edith Feeney, recorded on February 26, 1951 (deed book 979, page 396).

The following article appeared in a local paper (*Doylestown Intelligencer*, April 25, 1951) circulating in the neighborhood where Shirley and Bill owned their farm:

Shirley Booth's Home at Woodhill Undergoing Development

Wood Hill, April 24 – The transfer of "Wind Race Estate," of Mr. and Mrs. William Baker Jr., on the West side of the Doylestown Pike above Scully's Hill, which was sold before the death of Mr. Baker last winter, to Robert Feeney and Charles Judge, has been completed and the new owners are now developing it.

Mr. Judge resides in the modern frame house, facing Doylestown Pike, which was the residence of Francis E. Snively during his ownership of the place.

The stone farmhouse, which as restored and remodeled, by the Bakers for their home, has been sold with the barn and ten acres of land to Richard MacWhorter. Mr. MacWhorter is connected with the Diston's MFG. Co. of Philadelphia.

The land, south of the lane, along Doylestown Pike toward Dr. Deubler's, is being held for development into lots. Mr. Feeney will build a new residence along the south side of the maple-lined lane opposite the residence of Mr. Judge.

Mrs. Baker is Shirley Booth, now starring in *A Tree Grows in Brooklyn* on Broadway.

Their brief idyllic happiness would be no more. Shirley and 'her Bill' endured the rigors and enjoyed the pleasures of their dairy farm. This had been reportedly Shirley's happiest time in her life when she found herself at peace in her home. Though she solidified her credits as an actress during this period, she did not spend all of her energy pleasing radio and Broadway stage audiences. She simply loved playing the real-life role of a satisfied wife and homemaker!

Over twenty years later Shirley would still talk lovingly of Bill. But it was as if she regretted the toll that the farm had taken on Bill's life, and she seemed to maybe wonder what her life would have been if they had never moved to Bucks County. She told Penny P. Anderson, *TV Time and Channel*: "Being a farmer is the most underrated job in the world. It killed my husband, really, it did. There we were, two city slickers trying to work a farm. My husband had a history of heart problems and there were so many chores on the farm that were strenuous and foreign to him. It was too much."

Shirley never stopped remembering Bill, as when she told *The Saturday Evening Post*: "He loved the farm. He'd seen so much devastation during the war that he wanted to make things grow. But he did too much. He always did the heavy work while his helper drove the tractor...."

Nevertheless, it was Bill that did encourage Shirley out of retirement back to her first love – the stage. Shirley explained: "I tried so hard to take care of him and I think he pushed me back to work to get me off his neck."

With the dedication of a real trouper, Shirley would miss only two rehearsals before returning to the Broadway stage. Now widowed and heartbroken, it seemed that Shirley's work – the involvement in an exciting musical version of Betty Smith's *A Tree Grows in Brooklyn*, gave her the strength to live through this shock. Shirley would later say that "it hardly gave me time to think of anything else and, of course, I tried not to."

Shirley shared her deep love for her deceased husband and she revealed her compassionate personality to readers in Tricia Hurst's article, "An Intimate Portrait of Shirley Booth: Her Laughing Days . . . Her Lonely Nights." This interview, published in Shirley's *Hazel* days in the early 1960's, took a revealing look at Shirley's inner sadness when the performer's mask is off.

Shirley: "I miss my husband. Mourning for anyone or anything will not bring back the happiness. Life goes on, work goes on, you go on. . . ."

As to whether her feelings for her deceased husband affected her work, Shirley continued: "The answer is yes. I think I am more sympathetic to the characterization of Hazel than I would be, if he were alive. Hers is a more ribald and hearty sense of humor than mine, but I understand her not wanting people to feel sorry for her. She says and does things the rest of us would not have the nerve to say or do - although we would like to - but underneath is a kind woman who identifies with the Baxter family because it is the only one she has. Without them, she would be alone."

Shirley concluded: "I'm alone, but I can also be alone without being lonely. There is always something in your past that sets your attitude towards people and situations in your present. My husband would have been pleased with *Hazel*. I think he, above all others, would have understood my need to play her. Every day, when I walk on the set, I have a family . . . I belong to a family, and it has become a very real world to me."

What strikes one most when reviewing this short period when Shirley and Bill's lives were intertwined is to see her remarkable determination to go on performing after that beautiful period abruptly ended. How Shirley went on with her acting so soon after this heartbreaking misfortune is a fine testament to her character and her ability.

Kevin Minton, who interviewed and corresponded with Shirley in her twilight years, reflected on that sad time: "The loss of Mr. Baker hit her hard. Though neither fans nor critics would have guessed it, Miss Booth felt she sleepwalked her way through it."

The end of Shirley's marital bliss would be her darkest period in her personal life. Nevertheless, most interestingly she dealt with her heartbreak by making her performances in the show the brightest and the most upbeat in her entire life.

A *Tree Grows in Brooklyn*, as apparent from the surviving cast album, is arguably Shirley's best Broadway musical among the five that she did (*Hollywood Pinafore*, *By the Beautiful Sea*, *Juno*, and *Look to the Lilies*), and it is undoubtedly one of her most memorable accomplishments.

Finally, Shirley's unyielding perseverance and her ability to not allow her sorrows to overshadow her life, gave some closure to both her life with Bill, and her memories of country living down on their Pennsylvania dairy farm.

Although Shirley Booth never had any children with Ed Gardner or Bill Baker, she truly lived the rest of her life to the fullest. She remained single, but she never forgot her true love - Bill Baker.

Postscript

Later, after leaving Bucks County, Shirley would star (by her own choice) in only four Hollywood films, (*Come Back, Little Sheba, About Mrs. Leslie, Hot Spell, The Matchmaker*) and appear in a fifth (*Main Street to Broadway*).

Over the years, she had turned down many offers to make the film versions of some of her big Broadway hits, including *The Philadelphia Story, Tomorrow the World, The Desk Set*, and *The Time of the Cuckoo* (made as the film *Summertime*).

Her biggest fame would come later when millions would watch her on television in bringing to life Ted Key's *Hazel* from *The Saturday Evening Post* magazine panel. The show would run for five seasons and brought her two Emmy Awards. Unlike many shows from that era, *Hazel* holds up quite well and is generally still very funny, despite the fact that Shirley was already in her early sixties when the show premiered.

Shirley would make other television appearances, most notably in the 1966 Emmy-nominated production of Tennessee Williams' classic, *The Glass Menagerie*. As the voice of Mrs. Santa Claus in the 1972 holiday classic *The Year Without A Santa Claus*, Shirley Booth ended a long and quite prosperous career on a cheerful note. She spent her final years tending to her saltbox cottage property on Cape Cod, in Chatham, Massachusetts. She died on October 16, 1992 at the age of 94.

The Photographs and Paintings

The Photographs:

Shirley Booth's niece Leslie Sodaro provided forty photographs that were in family albums, along with three pictures of paintings (two by Bill and one by Shirley). All the photographs are printed in this book, except for the nineteen shots that were taken while shooting the 1952 film *Come Back, Little Sheba*. I chose not to publish them in this volume, saving them for a later in-depth study of that film.

The Paintings:

Unfortunately, the search for much of Bill and Shirley's artwork has not been successful. However, at least two of Bill's paintings do survive; namely, a winter scene looking outside a window, and a seascape. Only one of Shirley's paintings has been located for this book; namely, a snow scene.

Certainly, the three surviving paintings are not an adequate sample in order to assess their abilities. A cursory examination of them indicates that, as with most amateur artwork, Shirley and Bill's enthusiasm and effort exceeded a perfect professionalism and adeptness at it. Bill's work shows more skill – but some areas seem to drop off and are unfinished, as with the shadows of the trees on the snow. Perhaps if more samples of their work existed, a fairer assessment of the true extent of their skill would be evident. Their best work may be hidden away and undiscovered yet.

The Provincetown Art Association Benefit Auction in 2003 offered two paintings signed by Shirley Booth. The hammer prices recorded were $250 for the 9.5" X 7.5" "Still Life" oil painting on canvas, and $400 for the 7.5" X 9.5" "Harbor Scene" oil painting on board. This worked out to the highest price paid of $5 per square inch.

Please note that the photographs and paintings published here have not been seen by anyone, with the exception of family members and friends of Shirley Booth and Bill Baker. They are published here for the first time ever with the permission of Leslie Sodaro, Shirley Booth's niece and closest living relative.

> *My Aunt Shirley was a born storyteller, and not many people could top her. Her stories were always fleshed and accented. I do not remember any of them, but I do remember the adventure I went on with her in her stories. She loved to entertain.*
>
> - Leslie Sodaro

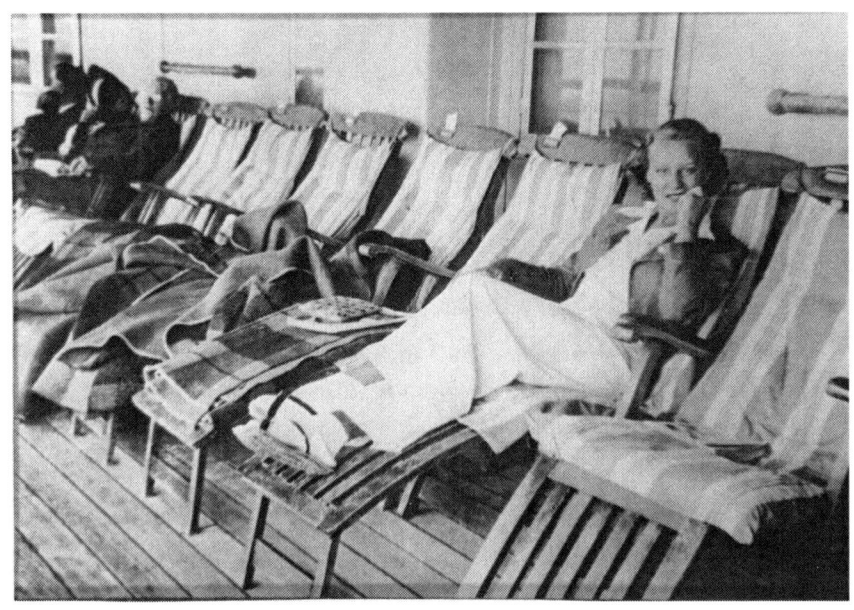

Shirley Booth lounging on a ship's deck: 4X6, B/W, Date and location unknown, circa 1930's. Photo courtesy of Leslie Sodaro.

> *Shirley had two farm mascots; a red-brown cocker spaniel named 'Baker's Candy,' and a boxer named 'Sugar.' Referring to 'Baker's Candy,' "I became a painter when my husband did that portrait of our dog. But he painted him with his tail drooping. I took the brushes and repainted the tail so it is standing defiantly up in the air. Since then I've been a determined artist."*
>
> — Shirley Booth (quoted in the late 1940's while married to Bill Baker)

Shirley Booth in her dressing room for the Broadway production of *My Sister Eileen*: 8X10, originally Sepia-toned, circa 1940. Shirley is seen holding her cocker spaniel. The dressing table has a picture of her then husband Ed Gardner. On the upper backside of the still, Shirley has inscribed: "My Sister Eileen taken by Dick Quine in dressing room." Another inscription on the left middle says: "can make copies belongs to Shirley must be returned to Shirley." Photo courtesy of Leslie Sodaro.

> *When Shirley Booth became engaged to marry Bill Baker, and was celebrating it with him at Sardi's, the theatrical restaurant, another actress sent over a note saying: 'You'll have to move, darling. You're so happy it gets in my eyes.'*
>
> - From "Lady with a Light"
by Jessyca Russell Gaver

Portrait of Corporal William H. Baker Jr. given to Shirley Booth: 8X10, originally Sepia-toned. The inscription in the lower right corner says: "To My darling with all my heart, Bill." Photo courtesy of Leslie Sodaro.

The Shirley Booth Pin-Up: wallet-sized, hand-colored, original photo in color on Front Cover, shown here in B/W. This is the most stunningly beautiful and treasured photograph of Shirley Booth in Leslie's family collection. Shirley gave this 1944 photograph to Bill while he served in the 100th Infantry Division during World War II. Photo courtesy of Leslie Sodaro.

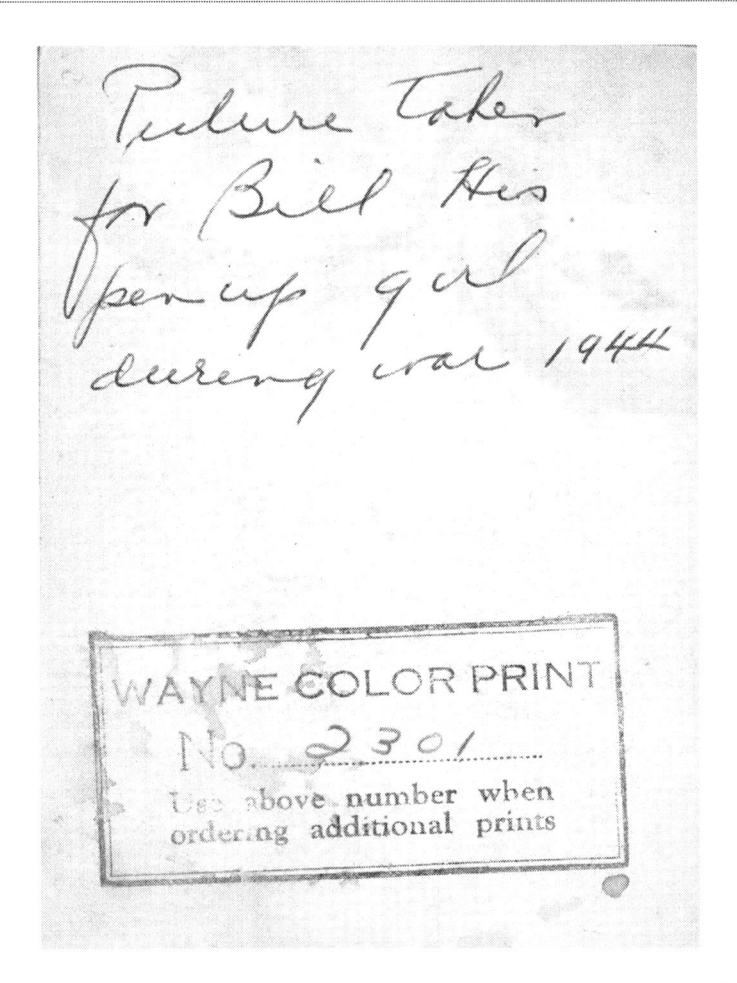

Backside of Pin-Up, Shirley Booth wrote "Picture taken for Bill His pin up girl during war 1944."

Twice in my life, I took sabbaticals from my career and I didn't mind the idleness a bit. I wasn't idle. I was a wife both times. I 'retired' once in Hollywood when I was married to Ed Gardner and he headquartered in Hollywood for radio. In my second marriage, we had a farm in Bucks County and I was up at 6 o'clock every morning.

- Shirley Booth

Shirley Booth admiring Bill's painting: 8X10, Originally Sepia-toned. Photo courtesy of Leslie Sodaro.

> *We thought it would be wonderful to live in the country but I get too emotional about killing chickens and selling calves for the market. I spent so much time painting the rooms in our house that I seldom got outside. I still love the feeling of the country – I guess this reflects a searching for peace I don't have in myself.*
>
> - Shirley Booth

Oil painting: Still Life Looking Outside Window in Winter, 9"x12". This painting resembles Shirley & Bill's property in Bucks County with twisted tree branches, by Bill Baker Jr. Photo courtesy of Leslie Sodaro.

> *I miss my husband. Mourning for anyone or anything will not bring back the happiness. Life goes on, work goes on, you go on....*
>
> - Shirley Booth

Oil painting: Seascape. 12"x10." Location unknown, by Bill Baker Jr., signed "William H. Baker."
Photo courtesy of Leslie Sodaro.

I love painting – painting ceilings and the kitchen walls. Also, oil painting. I do oils. It is the most absorbing occupation one could have. You can say this about an oil painting – it somehow never gets done. There's always one more touch you discover you can add.

- Shirley Booth, 1954

Oil painting: Snow Scene. 12"x10." This painting resembles Shirley & Bill's property in Bucks County, by Shirley Booth, signed "Shirley Booth 1954." Photo courtesy of Leslie Sodaro.

Merv Griffin:
  ...You were a singer first.

Shirley:
  No! I never first, last, or now!

Merv:
  Well, Shirley, I saw you in *A Tree Grows in Brooklyn* with Johnny Johnston....

Shirley:
  Yes, but you also saw Rex Harrison in *My Fair Lady*.

  - From *The Merv Griffin Show* (March 15, 1963)

Outside shot of Shirley Booth in costume for Broadway musical, *A Tree Grows in Brooklyn:* 3X5, B/W, 1951. Photo courtesy of Leslie Sodaro.

"*Well, I'll attempt anything you know. I don't always succeed, but what I lack in experience, I'll make up in enthusiasm!*"

- Shirley Booth, speaking about singing and dancing in *A Tree Grows in Brooklyn* on *The Merv Griffin Show*, March 15, 1963.

Outside shot of Shirley Booth in costume for Broadway musical, *A Tree Grows in Brooklyn*: 3X5, B/W, 1951. Photo courtesy of Leslie Sodaro.

By the Beautiful Sea

Fourteen 3"x5," B/W photographs. Although these photos are grainy and not professional quality shots, they depict a rare view of Shirley Booth on the Broadway stage during an actual production of *By the Beautiful Sea*, taken by a member of the audience. See the appendix for further details on this show.

Musical number: "I'd Rather Wake Up By Myself,"
By the Beautiful Sea, Broadway musical, 1954.
Photo courtesy of Leslie Sodaro.

Musical number: "I'd Rather Wake Up By Myself,"
By the Beautiful Sea, Broadway musical, 1954.
Photo courtesy of Leslie Sodaro.

By the Beautiful Sea, Broadway musical, 1954.
Photo courtesy of Leslie Sodaro.

By the Beautiful Sea, Broadway musical, 1954.
Photo courtesy of Leslie Sodaro.

By the Beautiful Sea, Broadway musical, 1954.
Photo courtesy of Leslie Sodaro.

By the Beautiful Sea, Broadway musical, 1954.
Photo courtesy of Leslie Sodaro.

By the Beautiful Sea, Broadway musical, 1954.
Photo courtesy of Leslie Sodaro.

By the Beautiful Sea, Broadway musical, 1954.
Photo courtesy of Leslie Sodaro.

By the Beautiful Sea, Broadway musical, 1954.
Photo courtesy of Leslie Sodaro.

Musical number: *"Hooray for George the Third,"*
By the Beautiful Sea, Broadway musical, 1954.
Photo courtesy of Leslie Sodaro.

Musical number: *"Lottie Gibson Specialty,"*
By the Beautiful Sea, Broadway musical, 1954.
Photo courtesy of Leslie Sodaro.

By the Beautiful Sea, Broadway musical, 1954.
Photo courtesy of Leslie Sodaro.

By the Beautiful Sea, Broadway musical, 1954.
Photo courtesy of Leslie Sodaro.

By the Beautiful Sea, Broadway musical, 1954.
Photo courtesy of Leslie Sodaro.

N. Y. MIRROR "Theatre-ticket ORDERGRAM" for "BY THE BEAUTIFUL SEA"

Make check or money order payable to:
TREASURER, MAJESTIC THEATRE
MAIL to . . . MAJESTIC THEATRE, 245 West 44th St., N.Y.C.

For the enclosed $ .... please mail .... tickets

At $ .... each. { Orch. / Mezz. / Balc. } For ....
 Day of week (give 3) Mat. or Eve.—Date of Month

Name ....

Street Address ....

City .... State ....

PRICE SCALE INCLUDES TAX
Wednesday Matinee—Orch. $4.03, Mezz. 3.45, Balc. 2.88, 2.30, 1.73.
Saturday Matinee—Orch. $4.60, Mezz. 4.03, 3.45, Balc. 2.88, 2.30, 1.73.
Eves. except Sun.—Orch. $6.90, Mezz. 5.75, 4.60, Balc. 3.45, 2.88, 2.30.

Copyright, 1949, N. Y. Mirror

Theatre ticket ORDERGRAM for *By the Beautiful Sea*, back.

WESTERN UNION

NA204 DL PD=BEVERLY HILLS CALIF 20 1043A FEB 20 PM 2 55
=MISS SHIRLEY BOOTH=
25 WEST 54 ST=

HAPPY TO INFORM YOU THAT YOU BEEN VOTED THE GOLDENGLOBE AWARD
FOR THE BEST DRAMATIC ACTRESS BY THE HOLLYWOOD FOREIGN
CORRESPONDENCE ASSOCIATION PLEASE KEEP IT SECRET UNTIL
PRESENTATION WHICH WILL BE MADE FEB 26TH STOP KNOWING THAT YOU
CANNOT BE HERE IN PERSON KINDLY DESIGNATE SOME OTHER MOTION
PICTURE STAR TO ACCEPT ON YOUR BEHALF STOP PLEASE REPLY CARE
OF 444 NORTH OAKHURST DRIVE BEVERLY HILLS CR 43476=
BERT REISFELD PRESIDENT HOLLYWOOD FOREIGN CORRESPONDENTS
ASSOC=

February 20, 1953 telegram informing Shirley of her Golden Globe Award for *Come Back, Little Sheba* film.

The Billboard Eleventh Donaldson Awards...Shirley Booth Best Performance by an Actress (Musical) For *By the Beautiful Sea*.

Views of the Bucks County property in 2010.

'Roadie' & Leslie Sodaro (Shirley Booth's Niece).
Photo Courtesy of Leslie Sodaro.

Credits

September 1946 – February 1951

The following credits are an incomplete list of Shirley Booth's accomplishments during the period when Bill and she bought their Bucks County farm until it was sold.

BROADWAY STAGE

December 11, 1946 - December 14, 1946: *Land's End*

January 16, 1948 - January 17, 1948: *The Men We Marry*

November 17, 1948 - December 24, 1949: *Goodbye, My Fancy*

November 7, 1949 - November 19, 1949: *Love Me Long*

February 15, 1950 - July 29, 1950: *Come Back, Little Sheba*

BUCKS COUNTY PLAYHOUSE STAGE

My Sister Eileen (August 25 – 30, 1947)

The Vinegar Tree (1948)

FILM

Strawhat Cinderella, 1949, Shirley appeared in this Justin Herman ten-minute short subject filmed at the Bucks County Playhouse

TELEVISION

January 22, 1949: *The March of Dimes Benefit Show*

August 28, 1949: *Celebrity Time*

January 1, 1950: *Celebrity Time*

RADIO

Circa 1946: *The Adventures of the Red-Feathered Man.* A short-run syndicated series of 13 episodes.

July 4, 1946 - September 26, 1946: *The Vaughn Monroe Show.* Shirley played her Dottie Mahoney character in an unknown number of broadcasts.

January 6, 1946: *Theater Guild on the Air.* "Three Men on a Horse," with Stu Erwin and Sam Levene.

January 18, 1946: *Pabst Blue Ribbon Town.* Starring Danny Kaye.

February 16, 1946: *Celebrity Club*, with Art Carney, Jackie Kelk and John Daly.

September 29, 1946 - March 23, 1947: *The Eddie Bracken Show.* Shirley played her Betty Mahoney character. 44 shows were broadcast between 1945 and 1947.

December 29, 1946: *Theater Guild on the Air.* "Broadway," with James Dunn.

Late 1947 - 1948: *Here's to Veterans.* Sponsored by the Veterans Administration, starring Vaughn Monroe, this series ran over 1,500 episodes and was broadcast at various days and times. Shirley appeared in an unknown number of episodes.

January 6, 1947: *The Cavalcade of America.* "The Woman on Lime Rock." Shirley played the lead of Ida Lewis with Les Tremayne.

February 9, 1947: *The Fred Allen Show.*

May 8, 1947: *Radio Reader's Digest.* "Uncle By's Two Wives," with Everett Sloane and Karl Swenson.

June 1, 1947: *Theater Guild on the Air.* "Three Men on a Horse," with David Wayne and Sam Levene.

October 5, 1947 - December 28, 1947: *The Fred Allen Show*. Shirley appeared in a number of episodes during this time.

October 23, 1947: *Radio Reader's Digest*. "The Bradlock Chest"

January 4, 1948 - June 27, 1948: *The Fred Allen Show*. Shirley appeared in a number of episodes during this time.

February 26, 1948: *Radio Reader's Digest*. "The Woman Detective and the Stolen Jewels."

CBS Recorded - April 9, 1948: *Our Miss Brooks*. Audition recording, not broadcast on radio. Shirley auditioned to play Miss Connie Brooks. Eve Arden landed the role.

April 12, 1948: *The Cavalcade of America*. "The Man Who Took the Freedom Train," with Eddie Albert.

June 13, 1948: *The Ford Theater*. "My Sister Eileen," with Ted de Corsia and Arthur Q. Bryan.

October 3, 1948 - June 26, 1949: *The Fred Allen Show*. Shirley appeared in a number of episodes during this time.

June 21, 1949 - September 14, 1949: *Hogan's Daughter*. Shirley starred in this short-run summer series.

October 29, 1949: *Kate Smith Calls*. Short-run series starring Kate Smith.

December 11, 1949: *The Theater Guild on the Air*. "Street Scene," with Karl Malden and Thelma Ritter.

March 26, 1950: *The Theater Guild on the Air*. "The Milky Way," with Danny Kaye.

February 4, 1951: *The Theater Guild on the Air*. "Come Back, Little Sheba," with Gary Cooper.

Appendix

The Farmhouse Today

The farmhouse passed from Shirley & Bill Baker to Mr. Richard MacWhorter in 1951. In October of 1967, the current owner, Dr. Bahij Madany purchased the home from Mr. MacWhorter. The seller told Dr. Madany that Shirley Booth once owned it. Dr. Madany provided this list of some of the improvements.

1. Planted 300 spruce trees to give privacy.
2. Much work done on the barn. A barn expert from Doylestown, Pennsylvania jacked it up with steel beams. An architect drew a supporting wall on one side, and shored up all of the barn's structure.
3. The high windows, which were broken by flying birds, were replaced with Plexi-glass, which is transparent, but not easily broken.
4. A fifty-year roof was placed on both the barn and the 3-car garage, which was imported from Hannibal, Missouri.
5. The slate roof was upgraded, and new solid copper gutters were installed.
6. On the barn, Dr. Madany pointed the stone on one side.
7. A second-level entrance to the barn was built so a car can drive into the second floor of the barn.
8. Heavy wood floor planking was installed on the second floor of the barn.
9. Extensive renovations were made on the house interior. The kitchen was renovated with new cabinetry, new steel sink, and a half bath. A new window was created in the dining room with custom-made raised paneling around the base of the windows. Wallpaper was placed throughout the house. The bathroom on the second floor was ren-

ovated with new bath, sink and wallpaper. All windows were replaced in 1998 with Norwood windows imported from Canada with the latest technology that has Argon gas in them.

10. The basement was purged and two geothermal units were installed to heat the house and provide hot water. A new high-velocity system was installed throughout the house without any ducts. It was installed by Unique A/C System (a leading company in the field).

11. Foam was sprayed under the roof to keep the house warm in the winter and cool in the summer.

By the Beautiful Sea

The following is an edited description of this Broadway musical, as originally found in *Love is the Reason for it All: The Shirley Booth Story*, published in 2008.

This 1954 show was the third musical comedy on Broadway of the five that she did. It previewed at Boston's Shubert Theatre beginning February 23 until March 13. From there, the show went to the Forrest Theatre in Philadelphia on March 16 where it played for three weeks before its Broadway debut. It opened at the Majestic Theatre and ran from April 8, 1954 to November 27, 1954.

Robert Fryer and Lawrence Carr produced, Marshall Jamison directed (the show began with Charles Walter directing), scenic designer Jo Mielziner created the colorful settings, Irene Sharaff designed the period costumes, and Donald Saddler did the choreography.

By the Beautiful Sea depicted the pleasures of Coney Island in the early 1900's. The nostalgic show included the excitement of Steeplechase Park's Tunnel of Love, the Old Mill boat ride, the Midway, and balloon parachuting.

Shirley played a blonde-haired vaudeville comedienne/performer named Lottie Gibson. She runs a boarding house several blocks from the beach. Her love interest is an aging, divorced, and impoverished Shakespearean actor named Dennis Emery (Wilbur Evans).

How convenient is it that both Emery's 17-year-old daughter "Baby Betsy" Busch (Carol Leigh) and Emery's promiscuous ex-wife are boarders in Lottie's house. As the story goes, Lottie gives Emery a check for a thousand dollars. When she realizes that her father used the funds in the bank already, Lottie must make the check good. An opportunity arises when Lottie attempts to win the money by doing a parachute jump.

Baby Betsy's mother has kept her from dressing her age in

order to keep her as a child star. With Lottie's assistance, Baby Betsy dresses as a woman, and then finds love. Baby Betsy is no longer opposed to her father and Lottie marrying by the finale. This frees Lottie to wed Emery.

Shirley explained: "I'm romantic and looking for a knight on a white charger. He seems so educated. I brush up on Shakespeare, a couple of scenes from *Macbeth*, and set that playwright back a hundred years. I sing five songs, including 'Thirty Weeks on the Road," a comic song about vaudeville. But I don't use a comedy voice as I did in *Tree Grows in Brooklyn*. And I dance a little. But not much. Everybody knows I'm not a dancer. I don't want people to think I'm saying – 'See how versatile I am.' I even go up in a balloon and come down in a parachute in this show. It's not a caricature of the period, it's a gentle satire."

On opening night in Boston, Shirley wanted to wear a blush pink gown, but zipper trouble forced her to wear a white dress. Many of the expensive clothes Shirley was asked to wear would not be in keeping with the character.

Shirley: "Most of those wonderful dresses I wear will have to go before the New York opening. I am supposed to be a vaudeville performer whose income will continue for a limited time. I am saving every cent I can afford for my theatrical boarding house. Lottie just wouldn't have been able to buy such a wardrobe. It is necessary for me to work too hard to overcome the handicap of all those expensive, exquisite costumes, in order to show how desperate I am to get hold of $1000. People can't believe that money means so much to me."

It has been said that Shirley had to wear unflattering clothes over the years on stage due to the kind of roles she played, until her Boston premiere of *By the Beautiful Sea*.

When fitting for the costumes, Shirley remarked to *Cue*: "This is the first show I've ever been pretty in." Later she explained: "Nothing but Mother Hubbard house dresses – and sloppy ones – for *Sheba*. In *Time of the Cuckoo* I had to wear the sort of conservative clothes a secretary would buy who supported her family for years, and who was having her first trip to Italy, now that she didn't have to pay out for them any longer. You can imagine how much I enjoyed the Sharaff gowns I am now wearing. But I have to think my characters as well as act them. I must never be conscious of my clothes being too decorative for the kind of woman I play."

Wilbur Evans as Shirley's love interest had experience on the stage already, unlike the leads in *A Tree Grows in Brooklyn*, Johnny Johnston and Marcia Van Dyke. Evans did the lead for *South Pacific* in London. Critic Saul Colin observed that not only did Evans fail in *By the Beautiful Sea*, but there's "the familiar and ugly banality of the background," and songs which were "neither distinguished nor original." Nevertheless, Colin praised Shirley Booth for her "talent and grace and oozing a lovable quality seldom found on the stage."

Among the cast of *By the Beautiful Sea* were Cameron Prud'homme as Lottie's irresponsible father, blues and jazz legend Mae Barnes as Lottie's maid Ruby Monk, Richard France as juvenile Mickey Powers, Anne Francine as Flora Busch, and child actor Robert Jennings as Half-Note.

As in Shirley's previous Broadway musical, *A Tree Grows in Brooklyn*, Arthur Schwartz composed the music, Fields wrote the lyrics, and Herbert & Dorothy Fields (brother and sister) wrote the libretto.

In referring to Shirley, *Theater Arts* (June 1954) noted: "She dances, hoisting her ample skirts to knee length on one occasion to run through a buck and a wing with little Robert Jennings that is elementary, old-hat and altogether captivating. And of course she acts with a range seldom seen on the musical stage, even though the content of this script would hardly tax the capacity of the Floradora girl."

New York Post critic Richard Watts, Jr. suggested that the book was at fault in that it interrupted the show; it should have been made "as a period vaudeville show without even the pretense of a libretto."

William Hawkins, *New York World Telegram*, saw Booth's outstanding performance: "She is adored because of her warm, personal quality, her contagious gaiety and the great good taste that keeps her from putting pressure on the audience...She is a million dollar value in show business."

Although the show is faulted for running out of steam by Act Two, "There is only one Shirley Booth, and this is her show," exclaimed John McClain of the *New York Journal American*.

"Friendly, unassuming and good-natured, honest with the other performers as well as with the audience, she makes a Coney Island holiday out of her part," concludes Brooks Atkinson of *The New York Times*.

Shirley kept in one of her fourteen scrapbooks a letter (dated March 23, 1954) from a physician who saw the production in Philadelphia. Dr. Arthur First found the "Lottie Gibson Specialty" number upsetting and in poor taste as contrasted to the nostalgia of the rest of the show.

First: "My wife, who feels the same as I do, told me to mind my own business, but even though I have delivered thousands of newborn babies, I still get a thrill out of the next one and fail to see the humor in the sadistic implications of an unwanted little baby."

In *By the Beautiful Sea*, Shirley sings "In the Good Old Summertime," as a countermelody to "Coney Island Boat;" her optimistic view of being single, the witty lament "I'd Rather Wake Up By Myself," and "Lottie Gibson Specialty." Wilbur Evans sings "Alone Too Long," "More Love Than Your Love," while Mae Barnes sings two showstoppers on love: "Happy Habit" and "Hang Up."

The Merv Griffin Interview

Here is the relevant portions of an interview that featured Merv Griffin interviewing Shirley Booth, which aired on March 15, 1963. Merv told Phil Gries that almost all of the NBC afternoon shows that he did from October 1, 1962 thru the end of March 1963 were erased. Phil was told this when he shot an interview with Merv in the late 1980's in Atlantic City for the series *Host to Host* with Steve Allen.

This transcript is derived from the only known tape in existence, courtesy of Phil Gries, Archival Television Audio, Inc.

Merv:
 (discussing Shirley with the audience) We're all delighted she accepted our invitation. She's – I don't think ever been interviewed on television before, and I know we're all curious about her because we all know her and love her on her NBC television series *Hazel*. But of course we know much about her before the series *Hazel*. She's an Academy Award winner for her fine performance in *Come Back, Little Sheba*. Other performances that you remember *My Sister Eileen, The Philadelphia Story, The Desk Set,* the musical *A Tree Grows in Brooklyn,* [Merv almost says 'Booklyn.'] Good singer too. Lots of other great plays and movies. And we're going to meet her today in person. So please greet her warmly, Miss Shirley Booth. (Musical interlude – mixed with audience applause.)

Shirley:
 (Sighs)

Merv:
 Boy, you look bright and chipper today.

Shirley:
 Oh, don't let my, colored uh suit fool you.

Merv:
Pretty blue.

Shirley:
I have a very bad throat.

Merv:
Have you?

Shirley:
Yes, I had no bad health in California, I come from New York, my native land, and I get a strep throat.

Merv:
Oh you're in style, because the whole place has it here.

Shirley:
I suppose so, but I hope I don't pass it on to anyone else. I'm sure no one else wants it. (Audience giggles)

Merv:
As you walked out the curtain today, as you walked out the curtain today, I don't know why flashing in my mind, because I've been talking about the Academy Award you won for *Come Back, Little Sheba*. But you made one of the greatest acceptances of an award ever seen. Do you remember your walk?

Shirley:
(laughs) Oh, that was a funny story, because it was between California and New York and Conrad Nagel was presiding here in New York and Ronald Coleman in California. And Conrad Nagel felt that we in New York were being slighted, they were sought of brushing us off. So he came to me just a little while before I went on, before the announcement came as to who was gonna win this category. And he said Shirley, "please, if you win, please say something. Everybody else had been saying Oh thank you, thank you

and away they go, so please say something." And I said, "Oh, Yes I will" because we want them to realize that something happens in N. Y. too – and the people are....

Merv:

(interrupts) and the announcements too...

Shirley:

...are animated yes! (Laughing) So, they announce my name Mr. Coleman said it and I was so anxious to get up there in a hurry, before they switched us off. I had a feeling that maybe they might switch us off before... and there they go! (Audience laughter)

Merv:

And the end of the story, she tripped and fell flat on her face. (Shirley laughing) That was a wrap. We'll be right back after station identification. (Musical interlude)

Commercial Break

Announcer:

From New York, *It's The Merv Griffin Show*! (Theme Music) (announcements of guests over the music) And now here's Merv!

Merv:

Thank you, Shirley Booth to my left, Marilyn Lovell, Louie Lomax, Peter Cook to my right, Frank Simms. (To Shirley): You've been, you've been away from us too long, Shirley, out there.

Shirley:

Well, uh, I'm very happy out there. But I'm one of these people that can adjust to any place I am.

Merv:

Well, what do you miss most about New York?

Shirley:
About New York? The people.

Merv:
The people?

Shirley:
Yes.

Merv:
The subways, the buses...

Shirley:
Oh, Yes...the a constant fermentation that goes on. It's wonderfully exciting. It's uh much more placid existence that we have there, but I don't think the beautiful country, and the nice clear skies, sunny skies all the time should be....

Merv:
Where?

Shirley:
In California. (Marilyn Lovell laughs at that remark along with Audience)

Merv:
Oh did it clear up! (to Audience laughter) A we keep reading...

Shirley:
It's really lovely there. It's perfectly beautiful.

Merv:
Somebody just came on the other day, that a - it was my home - native.

Shirley:
Of course, you're from San Francisco.

Merv:
Yes, Yes!

Shirley:
That's where I was going to retire 'til I went there a couple of times and tried to climb the hills. (Someone laughs)

Merv:
That is a problem.

Shirley:
That's a place to start when you're young and vigorous, not to retire.

Merv:
(To Peter Cook) Have you ever been there Peter?

Peter:
I've never been. I'd love to go.

Shirley:
Oh, it's very exciting. It's much like New York as it is any place, only it's a I think it's more than New York. Yes.

Merv:
Well, I think the people are a little warmer there.

Shirley:
They're wonderful. I played there. (Warm Applause)

Merv:
See, you got one warm applause.

Shirley:
(Laughs) I played there in *Come Back, Little Sheba* for quite a long time, a month anyway, and I have never played to such audiences. They were wonderful.

Merv:
It's a great theater town.

Shirley:
Just so enthusiastic, they love it!

Merv:
Have you seen Peter's show *Beyond the Fringe* yet? (Referring to Peter Cook)

Shirley:
Oh, yes, indeed! I .... I think it's brilliant. Just wonderful. Just when....

Merv:
(To Peter) How do you like that Peter when people look at you and say brilliant? Do you feel brilliant?

Peter:
No. I just feel stupid. That's all. I do.

(Shirley and audience laugh to his response)

Merv:
He's still mad at our practice of arresting performers.....

Shirley:
He's talking about the critics I've heard outside and although I never played in England, I did have one criticism in a picture that I played in with Burt Lancaster that was playing there. They said nice things about the performance, but they said I have a face like a cauliflower. (She laughs heartily with the audience)

Merv:
That's terrible. Who was it?

Shirley:
I don't know. I just accepted it. That's all. I didn't question it. I don't want to go any further, because maybe I thought he might be a little more revealing. (Audience ap-

plause)

... (Skipped the other guests speaking to Merv)

Shirley:
(referring to a critic in a discussion Merv had with Peter Cook)

Well, I'll forgive him anything because he's stage struck. I think that anybody that's stage struck in the profession, I love them. I don't care how they criticize it. They love the theater, and I think they do it because they care tremendously, and I never mind that sort of criticism, do you?

... (Skipped the other guests speaking to Merv)

Shirley:
Speaking about Charles Addams, I heard a very funny story from a young man named Phillip Barry, Jr. whose father was a very good friend of Charles Addams, and they came out to East Hampton I think it was, they were living there to play tennis one Sunday morning. He said he heard these terrible things about Charles Addams. He was quite young at the time, and this couple came and knew the wife had been modeled for this rather lank spare-looking woman that haunted houses. And uh, and so, he was expecting something frightening. Here came two charming young people, one with a butch haircut all in white and uh looking like collegians.

But he said, but as it got darker.... (Some one snorted)

Commercial Break

Merv:
We're on, we're talking about mutual friends that we have.

Shirley:
Yes!

Merv:
Shirley, at what age did you first walk on the stage?

Shirley:
Well, you mean amateur or professional?

Merv:
Either.

Shirley:
I – I was two and a half.

Merv:
I had a feeling that you started very young.

Shirley:
Well, this was in church you know - in a Sunday school program. I didn't really go on the stage professionally until I was twelve years old.

Merv:
What did you do then?

Shirley:
I played extra parts in the stock company in Hartford Connecticut (To applause)

Merv:
Were you....four warm applause (Referring to audience), were you...were. You were a singer first.

Shirley:
No! I never first, last, or now!

Merv:
Well, but I saw you in *A Tree Grows in Brooklyn* with Johnny Johnston....

Shirley:
Yes, but you also saw Rex Harrison in *My Fair Lady*.

Merv:
Did you play that part too? (Audience Laughter)

Shirley:
He didn't sing either.

Merv:
But it's a nice quality when actors sing....

Marilyn:
(She interrupts Merv) and dancers.

Merv:
(Continues) and dancers yes. Dancers more for the rhythm and actors have a nice way of....

Shirley:
(Interrupts) Well, I'll attempt anything you know, I don't always succeed, but uh, what I lack in experience, I'll make up in enthusiasm.

Merv:
I saw you sing two weeks ago on *Hazel*. It was a cute story, about all the ladies in town were gonna get together to have a benefit for the children's hospital.

Shirley:
Oh, Yes, Yes. I didn't see that. I happened to be in Mexico on vacation and I missed it, but I'm looking forward to it, but it was one of the things I was very anxious to see because this was the only thing ah in the insecure department is the singing, and so I like to listen.

Merv:
Weren't you just in Washington D.C. with our President?

(Referring to John F. Kennedy)

Shirley:
Yes. I went I was the....

Merv:
(He interrupts her) You didn't go down to clean the White House, did you?.

Shirley:
(Laughs) Oh, I didn't even have an offer. But I went, I was a chairwoman this year or rather chairman for the society of crippled children and adults, and so I went with a little girl.

Merv:
(interrupts her) For the Easter Seals.

Shirley:
For the Easter Seals, yes. And I went with this little girl to the White House and I must say that as Hazel and as Miss Booth I fell for the President, I think he's charming, perfectly charming, couldn't be anymore gracious and was very much surprised to find that he's quite tall, very slender and shy.

Merv:
And shy?

Shirley:
Very shy, Ah.... We were sort of assembled out in the hall. He had immediate business that he had to attend to, so we waited a little while and finally he opened his door and just you know and said in his most friendly voice "Well come on in." Very friendly way. We went in. And he was very nice

to the little girl. And probably if you saw the newsreel you'd know that she didn't like facing the camera. She was very much afraid of the flashlight, she thought they were going to flash all the time. So we were concerned, mainly concerned with having her to turn around so the cameras could see her. And a finally we got her in the chair, and she felt more secure I think because she was a little nervous on the floor with her crutches. And she said to the President, "I went to the Senate yesterday and the Senator gave me a pen with his name on it." And the President said "Oh goodness that's just what I was gonna give you." (Laughter). So, he rang, a pushed a button under his desk and out came his secretary with a lovely bracelet - a medallion with a PT boat on it. She was so happy, oh well I would have been happy. I thought maybe I'd get one but I didn't. (Audience laughter)

Merv:
That was a sweet story, sweet story. How long are you going to be in New York.

Shirley:
I'm leaving on Tuesday.

Merv:
Now, do you have more *Hazel* films to do?

Shirley:
Oh yes, oh yes (While she is starting to explain this Merv overlaps by commenting "Are you that far ahead.") I'm filming on the 8th of April, and I go on until July and then I hope to get up to the Cape, where I have a cottage, and where I really work like Hazel. I work like a field hen up there.

Merv:
Oh, you have a cottage up in Cape Cod?

Shirley:
Yes.

Merv:
What's the city up there?

Shirley:
Chatham.

Merv:
Ah ha Oh that's pretty up there.

Shirley:
It's an old house and I've done a lot of things in it and I'm very ambitious. I wallpaper and refinish furniture. And I make rock gardens, and I lift sod. I have no sense at all. I pick up anything and carry it - Powerful Katinka.

Merv:
Ah that's nice. That's nice!

Marilyn:
That's a trait of your birth sign.

Merv:
Oh, but there she goes again. Tell us about Miss Booth.

Marilyn:
Well, we're both Virgo-ites.

Merv:
Well I use that in my garden. (Gets laughs from audience) Oh yes, It's very, it's very good.

Shirley:
You forgot one thing.

Merv:
I hate to be under that sign though.

(Skipped the other guests speaking to Merv)

Merv:
I never heard Shirley Booth tell a joke.

Shirley:
You haven't?

Merv:
No (laughingly). What's the story?

Shirley:
Well, this is the story about Cardinal Spellman sitting in his study one day and the knock comes on the door, and a young priest comes in, and he said, "a Father, our Lord is here." And he said, "of course my son, our Lord is everywhere." He said, "No Father, he's in the next room." And he said, "my son you've been working too hard. You say fifty Hail Mary's and take a nap." (Audience laughs) So he went back to his folio, another knock came at the door, and another priest stood there. And he said, "Father, our Lord is here." He said, "Yes my son, this is our Lord's house." He said. "No father he's in the next room." And he said, "Uh, my son go in peace, I have work to do."

So this went on until four priests had knocked on the door, and finally Cardinal Spellman thought something ought to be done about it. So he folded his folio and went out in the hall, and there in front of a certain door, were four priests gathered in trepidation and fear, and they said, "He's in there Father, he's in there." So he opened the door, and there stood our Lord in his white robe and halo, and his hands raised in benediction. He closed the door quickly and the priests said, "Father, what shall we do?" He said, "Look busy!" (Audience laughs and claps)

Merv:
That's five for you. (Shirley laughs) Cute story, Shirley. Shirley Booth, thank you so much. We will forever and a day watch *Hazel* on Thursday nights on NBC.

Shirley:
Thank You.

Merv:
And I can't thank you enough for coming on this show.

Shirley:
Well, I wouldn't have missed it.

Merv:
You're very cute. That's Shirley Booth. Thank you Marilyn Lovell. Look up some more information and come back anytime, and to Louie Lomax, I certainly advise everybody to read *The Negro Revolt*. Excellent book. Thank you, Thank you Peter Cook, best to you - in all of your endeavors and there are many of them. You're a busy young man and a bright one. Thank you. And we'll see you all on Monday, when Dody Goodman, Sam Cook, and Betty Friedan will be joining us. And I understand quite an intriguing fashion show. Have a very pleasant weekend. Happy St. Patrick's Day, thank you and good afternoon. (Ending Music) Announcer closing remarks……

(Closing Music)

SHOW END

"There is a land of the living and a land of the dead and the bridge is love, the only survival, the only meaning."

- Thornton Wilder, *The Bridge of San Luis Rey*

Love is the Reason for it All

The Shirley Booth Story

By Jim Manago
with Radio Research by Donna Manago

Foreword by Ted Key

$24.95 plus postage

www.bearmanormedia.com